Endorsements

LinkedIn proves that building strong, mutually beneficial relationships, which are at the core of every successful leader's network, can be done in 5-Minutes a day!

David L. Hancock
Founder, Morgan James Publishing

If you aspire to influence your network, Lori's and Joe's personable approach will draw you in and inspire new ideas for you to achieve extraordinary results.

Charles P. Garcia
2019 Harvard University Advanced Leadership Initiative Fellow

Lori's and Joe's long histories of building bridges for others across the LinkedIn network make them super-qualified to offer these actionable tips and strategies for success. Read it now!

Joel Comm
New York Times Best-Selling Author

LinkedIn shows you how to navigate the nuances of the most powerful online networking tool of our day to give you a competitive advantage. Take it!

Scott Friedman
Global Speaking Fellow

Lori and Joe focus on a critical platform for long-term success, and how to use it efficiently. Read this book AND... Network, and build Communities because... a Network gives you Reach, but a Community gives you Power. #RonR #NoLetUp!

Ted Rubin
Best-Selling Author

I followed the steps in this book and quickly was getting several calls a week expressing interest in me. Some of the greatest value Ruff and Frankie offer is the emphasis on introspection: stopping to see where I have created value, then communicating it in an appealing way.

My new role is fantastic. I connected to it through LinkedIn. I couldn't have found it without Lori Ruff and Joe Frankie.

Torrence Smith
Regional Continuous Improvement Manager,
Recycling Industry

Ruff and Frankie make implementing their tenets easy and fun to carry out. I was quickly successful effectively marketing myself to the world professionally. And I *Stand Out!* Passive networking increased monthly search appearances to daily resulting in many calls

Read this book cover to cover. Implement everything discussed inside. You will find answers and create new and renew old professional relationships with the help of your LinkedIn network.

Brian Laszakovits
Senior Network Engineer and Program Manager,
Commercial Cable Industry

Lori Ruff showed me that my LinkedIn profile is my personal brand and that I need to stay on top of stewarding its content: *not just on my profile but connected to my profile*. Done well, I can use it for communication and to build bridges to people and companies for business and career development.

This book is a must read to build a more meaningful network, nurturing long-lasting relationships, and staying in touch with businesses, colleagues, and friends. Thanks for such a fun but practical and comprehensive guide!

Scott McKenzie
Global Consultative Sales Executive, Business Replacement Lighting
ProductsTeaching Parent High Risk Residential Youth Home

Lori and Joe keep you up to date on best practices for routinely growing your LinkedIn network and investing in relationships to deliver more opportunities. They unpack all the best practices of the pros in one place to help you grab and go, serving up to-dos with how-tos with a side of conversation and case study so every one hears a message they can swallow.

Mike O'Neil
The LinkedIn Rockstar
Top 50 Social Media Influencer
Speaker, Trainer, Author, Futurist

Ruff and Frankie deliver a work for progress: yours! Their book is not only fun and entertaining, it has more good ideas in it than you'll be able to use. Maybe you'll be able to use them all but it'll take some effort. If you DO use all the ideas, expect to show up online where people can find you.

Tim Patterson
The "Go To" Tradeshow Guy for Exhibits
Author, Vlogger, Podcaster, Blogger

I'd done all the basics, but really nothing to stand out. The tips in *LinkedIn* are invaluable… Get a copy and read it in front of your computer—you'll be amazed at the tiny but important behind-the-scene items recommended to be more effective!

Phyllis Zimbler Miller
Military Fiction Author
Amazon Breakthrough Award Semifinalist

I found myself floundering on LinkedIn: with effectively finding clients, or what, where, or how to post to efficiently engage. The 5-Minute Drill gave me concrete, easily digestible suggestions that I could implement for immediate success.

Andrew Cameron
Graphic Breeze and Camera Breeze, Founder
Responsive Global Brand Design & Stock Images

LinkedIn

for Executive
Networking Success

Lori Ruff
Col (Ret.) **Joe Frankie III**

NEW YORK

LONDON • NASHVILLE • MELBOURNE • VANCOUVER

LinkedIn

The 5-Minute Drill for Executive Networking Success

Published in New York, New York, by Morgan James Publishing. Morgan James is a trademark of Morgan James, LLC. www.MorganJamesPublishing.com

ISBN 9781642794540 paperback
ISBN 9781642794557 eBook
Library of Congress Control Number: 2019931587

Cover Design by:
Andrew Cameron
www.GraphicBreeze.com

Interior Design by:
Chris Treccani
www.3dogcreative.net

Morgan James is a proud partner of Habitat for Humanity Peninsula and Greater Williamsburg. Partners in building since 2006.

Get involved today! Visit
MorganJamesPublishing.com/giving-back

Project Manager, Marketing Consultant, Case Study Researcher and Writer: Bob Bowden

Copy Editor: Lori Ruff

Developmental Editors: Bob Bowden, Cliff Glickman, Kim Keyes, and Neli Andersen

LinkedIn© is a copyright of LinkedIn Corporation

Neither the authors, nor editors are affiliated with LinkedIn in any way, except as may be described herein. Rather they work to support the member community now with over 600,000,000 professionals worldwide.

RockTheWorld™, RockLinkedIn©, and The LinkedIn Rockstar® are owned by RockTheWorld Media Group. Lori Ruff is formerly affiliated with the Group as an executive, author, and speaker.

For information about special bulk purchase discounts and/or co-branded sponsored-edition prints, please contact lori@loriruff.com

"A hundred times a day I remind myself that my inner and outer life are based on the labors of others, living and dead, and that I must exert myself in order to give in the same measure as I have received."

Albert Einstein

"The goal of professional networking should be nurturing your network to develop your career, business or personal objectives or advancing your community, which comes back to you when your need is indeed greatest in the full circle of reciprocity."

Bob Bowden

"In different places, you can wear different clothes, but you don't change who you are. When you fight to be different inwardly to fit the situation rather than to adapt outwardly, that's when you come across as one who is not who they claim to be—untrustworthy."

Lori Ruff

"You always are who you are; at different times you have different personas. You might talk to professional Lori Ruff when she's a speaker just off the stage, or you might catch her when she's talking about her daughter and see her as a mother. Yet always, she is Lori Ruff."

Joe Frankie

Dedication

By Lori Ruff

This book has come out of me because of the champions God has placed in my life.

When I was still in grade school Daddy came home with news that someone had found their dream job. I asked him how. *"**He knew somebody who introduced him to the right person**."* So, I asked, *"**Daddy, how do I get to know somebody?**"*

I truly believe that's when my interest began in meeting people on purpose, with integrity, with an expectation that NOT every person you helped would also help you. As Mr. Rogers pointed out, "every human being has value" and Daddy liked to add, "you just needed to know how to look for it!"

I was blessed to have Daddy to provide advice and guidance until Oct 2, 2012, always with hope that I would heed his advice. I continue to be astonished at how clearly his voice rings in my ears, often and loudly enough to help me navigate the professional and personal relationships that are important to me.

I carried this idea of helping others and paying kindness forward to my professional and my personal life and continued the practice with people online as well. So, in everything I do and in everything I am, I thank God for Daddy and Mom and for the influence and example they have been to me throughout my life, and my sisters Terri and Patty, too.

On May 11, 1991, God granted our prayers for a good Christian daddy for my daughter and a good Christian husband for me. The only stipulations our daughter put on her prayers: this guy had to have skin on, and he had to be the same guy!

Oh, the innocence of youth! And Steve was both those things and more. He was the tether that held my sail safely grounded allowing me to soar freely without fear. Until January 30, 2018, when, like Daddy, he got a better offer he just couldn't refuse!

So, now the two most important men in my life are home and I long for the day I will join them. But until God calls me home, I will continue my work to impact people who impact others, thereby amplifying my effect on the world. My "verb" in a word, is "Because I Love."

If you haven't discovered your verb, I encourage you to listen to Alex Mandossian's "Discovering Your Verb" podcast on All Selling Aside.

Because I love and am gifted with giants, it is to my God, my Daddy and my giants that I dedicate this book.

Acknowledgments

By Lori Ruff

I thank God for the gift of **Steven Ruff** who always knew I had to fly and was always proud to be my anchor.

I thank my former partner, **Mike O'Neil**, The LinkedIn Rockstar. We were so driven and so pushed each other beyond our limits. We took risks and tried new things going right to the edge of the cliff so we'd know how to help you navigate safely around it.

I thank **Olivier Taupin**, founder of some of the largest groups on LinkedIn; **Charlie Garcia**, the living embodiment of what a global leader can achieve with the full benefit of LinkedIn; **Ken McArthur** for the Impact he is having on so many people I care about across the nation and the globe; **Joel Comm** for his authentic heart and humble spirit, his willingness to recognize the magic in the common man standing right next to him, and to celebrate it… (You Inspire Me!); and, **Jorge Hermida** for four amazing years of growth and opportunity through production of RockTheWorld™ with LinkedIn radio. There are so many giants, those I know and those who helped me but never said so…their names would fill a book—and I'm so grateful to each one.

And, Joe and I are both indebted *beyond words* to the incredible, **Robert "Bob" Bowden III**, for his never failing ability to answer our calls or emails requesting help for research, phrasing, marketing, even some pinch writing, scheduling posts, running analytics, and generally cheering us up whether we need a smile or just a great stupid joke. Without Bob and without the masterful talent and caring dedication of **Andrew Cameron**, not only our designer but also our friend, we'd still be writing and out shopping for cover art!

Acknowledgments

By Joe Frankie

In the past half-decade, I have coached 500+ executives and transitioning military personnel on how to better use LinkedIn to accomplish their goals and better merchandise themselves. This is just a natural extension of what I did as a senior officer in the military—coach and develop junior officers.

Over the years, many people I've worked with have encouraged me to write a pamphlet or eBook on the tips, rules of the road and storytelling I've used to help them on saddling their LinkedIn horse for their journey. This 5-Minute Drill is the culmination of that mission. Little did Lori or I know we would be awarded a GOLD (Career Development) and SILVER (Business) Awards in Daniel Poynter's 2017 Global e-Book competition.

I thank my bride of 40+ years, Karen, for her patience and selflessness in helping create the time to work on this book and coach executives and former service members on LinkedIn or their transition from the military to the private sector.

"We get what we want in life by helping others get what they want in life."

Tom Hopkins

Table of Contents

Foreword

We asked Lana Khavinson, a LinkedIn Expert and Digital Business Marketing Professional to share her thoughts about the importance of representing your professional persona online and in particular, on LinkedIn. Lana is a former LinkedIn Marketing Manager for Company Pages, Small Business, and LinkedIn for Good products

Regardless of your industry, company size, or job function, LinkedIn is an invaluable tool for all professionals, especially those in leadership positions. With over 500 million professionals around the world, LinkedIn has a network of people and resources that can help any executive become that much more successful.

Executives have found LinkedIn an incredible place to connect with fellow leaders, mentors, specialists, investors, and more. By providing easy tools for engaging with the LinkedIn network, an executive can quickly find the exact person that they need to reach. Given the content that flows daily through LinkedIn, leaders can always feel in the know and ready for the next challenge.

I've personally seen some incredible examples of business leaders using LinkedIn to build out peer networks, partnerships, and rich communities. In fact, one leader that I worked with was able to find a business partner by engaging in a shared group. Through that partnership, they were able to double their business leads in under one year. What's been even more exciting is seeing leaders speaking up on important topics taking place in their industry and the economy at large. Not only have they been able to build their executive and corporate brand, but they've created a community of followers that are now able to learn and thrive.

LinkedIn is all about creating economic opportunity for every member of the global workforce. The connectivity and ease with which leaders can engage with one another and the community at large not only help business but creates the foundation for a better world.

I can't wait to see what you all do with *The 5-Minute Drill*—it will no doubt be incredible and inspirational.

— Follow Lana on

LinkedIn: linkedin.com/in/lanakhavinson

Lana Khavinson *is currently Product Marketing Lead - Groups at Facebook.*

She was formerly at LinkedIn a Product Marketing Leader: LinkedIn for Good; LinkedIn Groups; Small Business Resource Center; and LinkedIn Company Pages. And, previously served Intuit and Yahoo both in Online Marketing & Mobile Development.

"Begin with the end in mind."

Dr. Stephen R. Covey

The "5-Minute Drill for Networking Success" Outline

We are going to do something radical here and give you the book in a nutshell, right up front, in two pages. Why? Well, we're either stupid or stupendous. We just will not know for sure until you pass the "stup-", so come on in and try us out.

Does This Really Work? **If you must ask, you probably need the book.** But ask yourself, "Are you ready to start looking for renewed joy with a new audience or a fresh conversation that will spark your interest and electrify your morning routine?

It starts now.

Prepare. Set a timer. For best results, use your mobile device's timer for your entire drill or each section. As you find your groove, use the stopwatch and hit Lap as you begin the next step and the next, so you know how much time you spend on each. Don't be afraid to modify the steps to suit you but hold off on that until you have completed at least ten days on the standard drill to give each step a fair shot.

1) Open LinkedIn and scroll down your home page, full of updates and activity from personal connections and companies you follow. (**2 minutes**)

   a) Like and Comment on 5 - 20, depending on the size of your network and the length of your "Drill." Remember it is important for you to be seen as an intelligent human that cares about the people and the business. Don't leave throw-away comments, rather take a couple more seconds to invest in something a bit more intellectual and competent.

    b) Be sure to take note of any immediately beneficial content or connections you come across. Write them down and bookmark the page.

    c) But do NOT stop your drill! It is essential that you use your drill time on the drill—it's only Five Minutes! And you might miss an even bigger deal if you quit the race too early.

2) Visit 3-5 groups each day and find 3-5 active discussions on which you can make intelligent comments. (**2 minutes**)

    a) People who post comments to those discussions will be heard and make the original posters feel heard. Onlookers in the group will take notice of you as well, increasing your visibility from others "in the room", making you the topic of conversation.

    b) Once you get a feel for what engages that audience, post engaging content! Don't be afraid to ask for opinions!

3) Look for and connect with at least two to five individuals every day. No executive must think long to come up with realistic options representative of at least two of the following categories. Be sure to send them a note if possible, either with the invite, via email, or even text. If you send the invite after you meet, let them know it's coming; if before, give them a taste of what to expect. (**1 minute**)

    a) Colleagues and peers.

    b) Mentors and those whose work you admire.

    c) Professionals you might meet at a conference and engage.

That's it. Notice how your network grows, your views increase, your phone rings more, and, particularly as you refine the topics of your conversations, you become a recognized thought leader in your industry and for your area of expertise!

"The quality of your attention determines the quality of other people's thinking."

Nancy Kline
Pioneered "The Thinking Environment"
Best Selling Author, Keynote Speaker
Time To Think, More Time To Think, and *Living With Time To Think*
Corporate and Ivy-League Educator

Where and How to Begin

Yes, the book is about the 5-Minute Drill, and the basics are easy to find. But the authors have more gems to share. Keep your eyes open. For those ready to find more, look past the basics and you'll find more in the stories we share, in the resources, and in the case studies and practical applications.

If you are already on LinkedIn, well versed in the various areas of the platform, and you don't need to be convinced about the value of being here, skip around. But you don't have to. We made it a quick read on purpose!

A quick skim of these first two introductions will provide insight into why the authors got actively involved in networking on LinkedIn and how they have benefitted from doing so. It is stories, after all, that give us the greatest perspective into any environment.

Even if LinkedIn is not new to you, you likely picked up this book because you are hoping to use it in a new way. So, what's the harm in investing in a couple of quick short stories to gain—or regain—perspective?

If you have not started or created an account, then stop and read this before you do anything else. It will help you decide the best way to proceed to meet your own goals and objectives. If you're still not sure what to do, give Joe Frankie a call. His number is on his profile! Of course, Lori will be around to help you, too.

Connect with Lori:
www.linkedin.com/in/loriruff

Connect with Joe:
www.linkedin.com/in/joefrankieiii

Networking on LinkedIn

With Lori Ruff

The LinkedIn Diva joined LinkedIn on July 14, 2005, upon receiving her third invitation. Yes, I even needed to be prodded a few times to look at the then new, self-described "Professional Network" site. At first, I thought it just a nice step above Plaxo, which at the time was useful to stay connected with your professional network. Though in a few short years of active networking in my local region, I'd crushed the 1,000-connection limit Plaxo imposed.

Yet, after I accepted the invitation, created a login, and added the expected contact information and professional affinity, LinkedIn continued to ask for more information, like someone you meet at a BNI luncheon who genuinely wanted to get to know you.

Beyond "My Title at My Company" and the date I began, it wanted a position description in a free-form text field that provided plenty of room, if not to be verbose, then at least tell a great story or two of how I addressed and solved a critical problem at work!

"I felt as if I had entered a large networking event and was moving from person to person without ever leaving my office!"

Lori Ruff

Then "Former Employers", "Education", and "Volunteer Experience" were offered as well as a few more fields in which professional people involve themselves. Yet the fields that struck me most were the "Summary" and "Specialties" options.

I considered what I might include: a summary of my work, who I was as a professional, and what I wanted when networking in this new environment from the people I might meet here. That phrase struck me as the thought went through my mind: *from the people I might meet here.*

Who might I meet here? What people were attracted to this environment and how would they find my profile?

I could easily find the profile of the person whose invitation I had accepted. I also quickly found the two other invitations I had been sent in my inbox. It was easy to accept them and to view their profiles. As I viewed each profile, I could easily find others who had connected to these professionals as well as those who had recommended them. I felt as if I had entered a large networking event and was moving from person to person without ever leaving my office!

I also saw the power of using this *easily* updated profile as a dynamic online resume in the days of Word 2000, from which people could not easily convert their resumes to the PDF files that recruiters and hiring managers began requiring by email. The easy updates allow you to make not only instant career changes, but regular updates *relevant* to your professional presence via post or article.

Staying top of mind is the reason many people wanted to meet at the water cooler, the coffee shop, daytime or evening networking events.

I was in the Charlotte, NC region—a US Airways hub where Textiles and Tobacco were once king of the economy—

resumes, electronic resumes, and an easy way to apply for jobs was certainly a dire need.

At the time, I owned and operated Document Solutions of NC, a regional business offering on-demand project support, computer training, writing, and resumes. Helping people find employment while simultaneously assisting businesses and their recruiters to find the people was an interesting dynamic. One that allowed me to refine the way I recommended to audiences and private clients how to represent themselves appropriately yet truthfully.

They had to now align online profiles with sometimes multiple versions of paper resumes representing expected skills, attributes and abilities companies sought. Before 2005 was over, I and my team had added more than 300 professional profiles onto this new, powerful networking platform. That's an average of three a day in under six months!

"It can be assumed, like every professional, that YOU have experience; I want to hear the story of YOUR experience; I want to read your profile and feel like I have met YOU."

Lori Ruff

Along my journey, circa 2008, I partnered with Mike O'Neil, The LinkedIn Rockstar (now you know where my Diva title originated!). He was tackling his first book when we met and we joined forces—in business, too. We decided to make two books. "RockTheWorld™ with Your Online Presence: Your Ticket to a Multi-Platinum LinkedIn Profile" and the second on the topic of LinkedIn to empower sales.

Although long before "Social Selling" became a thing. Mike had developed formal training on using LinkedIn to empower sales success, we continued to refine and use it to teach salespeople, recruiters, and marketing teams how to use LinkedIn to impact their bottom line ever since.

Individually and together, we also trained and inspired over 150 other LinkedIn and social media trainers, speakers, and consultants, only a few of whom include: Holly Clere, Joel Comm, Grant Crowell, Lissa Duty, Petra Fisher, Marc Freedman, Brad Friedman, Melony Dedaro, Shawn Elledge, Richard Geasey, Rob Gibbs, Jeffrey Gitomer, Glen Gould, Chuck Hester, Lewis Howes, Jeff Kaye, Chris Kiersch, Chris Kovak, Holly Kolman, Deb Krier, Nancy Laine, Chad Massaker, Ken McArthur, Ian McCleary, Rob Melendez, Jeff Mills, Nile Nickel, Lucinda Ruch, Haydn Shaughnessy, Paul Slack, Doug Stern, Terry Sullivan, and Olivier Taupin.

We even influenced Joe Frankie III, giving him our structure to help veterans transition to civilian life. He believed, as we did, that the first step for transitioning to a new chapter is authentically representing yourself and your skills accurately to a new audience in their own language. And... drum roll please, helping veterans believe, they too, are worthy of recognition for their skills, talents and abilities gained through military experience that now translates into the public domain.

Where, in 2008, I encouraged people to speed their traditional networking by practicing a few routine drills 1-3 times each day on LinkedIn, you can now work, network, and connect the way you once did only in a weekly 90 minute face to face networking event.

Take 5!

Staying top of mind is the reason many want to meet. Doing so virtually amplifies your efforts exponentially.

Bear in mind, more so than in person, everything an executive does in the virtual space will contribute to how people perceive them as a person. In addition to what you post, be mindful also to how you post, how often you post, and where you post. Everything you do online will reflect on the entirety of your persona… everything!

In 2014, I began representing the new LinkedIn story on stage, helping people already sold on being there to truly represent who they are as people not just professionals. They were also committed to connecting, to selling, to hiring, to growing, to learning, to volunteering…. I believe the exponential impact of LinkedIn on one's life truly begins to be felt when others introduce you without prompting to someone in their inner circle, or when an executive you have helped embrace the power of this community asks you to help their son or daughter enter it, too.

As LinkedIn has changed—from a place to network, find a job, hire, sell, research schools, or to follow companies or your favorite colleagues, industry leaders or international newsmakers—the perception of the marketplace has evolved as well.

Now do whatever you feel you can through the massive networking here and its dynamic sister sites tied to LinkedIn's Economic Graph:

- LinkedIn For Good where people who have hours of trade skills and board service desires are paired with non-profits who need skilled volunteers and board members.

- LinkedIn Learning for individuals who need a skill to advance at work to online learning for faculty, staff and students at colleges and universities, governments, and elearning for business managers and leaders or to "upskill your entire workforce" as the needs of the marketplace more rapidly change.
- LinkedIn Social Impact to support for the military and veteran community the tools and networking opportunities to create meaningful career connections to help stand out to America's employers.

During my work over the years, I'd had several people, including more than a couple of LinkedIn employees, encourage me to write a book - *Five Minutes a Day to Networking Success on LinkedIn.* So, as I was finally settling into my role as the first Chief Branding Officer for ALPFA (Association of Latino Professionals For America), Joe called and said he had been promoting my first book. As we enjoyed a few long conversations, I realized this book would not be complete without his input.

His experience as a combat commander and executive recruiter as well as a veteran transition mentor inspired me. And it was his incredible patience and tenacity that got this book to the finish line and into your hands!

"Honor the generosity you have received and enjoy the privilege of giving to others and paying it forward."

Ileana Musa
International Banking & Lending
Morgan Stanley

Networking on LinkedIn

With Col. (Ret.) Joe Frankie III

My first day of officially "retired from active duty" was on July 1, 2004. Around that time, I was talking with a friend about networking and she sent me an invitation to join this site called LinkedIn saying it will prove to be a powerful tool. I accepted her advice and allowed her to nudge me forward.

Still, I thought this was a lot of information to be open on the web. After 30 years of military service, I was not of a mind to share so much of my life in such a public way. Operational security was ingrained in every fiber of my being. I hesitated; not doing much with it until a few months later.

Finally, I filled out my experience and positions on LinkedIn. I began to reach out to my contacts, but I couldn't get anyone else from the military to join my network.

"The work world is screaming for people who can solve problems. It is about metrics—qualitative and quantitative."

Joe Frankie

In a conversation, I spoke with LinkedIn co-founder Konstantin Guericke, and he shared that his initial goal for the platform was to replicate a small German community where everyone knew everyone else. He was an initial advocate of very small, quality networking. He is a self-proclaimed "biggest fan of LinkedIn!"

From that conversation, what convinced me to trust the concept of LinkedIn, was that I had grown up in a small town in Texas in a very similar environment. Secondly, I had been stationed in Germany near some very small communities, and I understood the concept he conveyed.

I realized LinkedIn was a virtual, online method to create community. In the small town where I grew up, you knew all the people, or most of the people. You understood these people because you shared common interests and culture.

In the same way, I used LinkedIn to create a community of people with shared interests and values important to me. LinkedIn became a way for me to create a culture. My culture reflected the values and interests important to me.

Today my community of connections are all joined by common threads of an industry, business, or shared experiences that I've had.

Each person's profile–through their connections, their interests, their groups–whether they know it or not, will convey the community in which they are most comfortable. Be it large or small; if it is a place where everyone is a known and trusted connection; is it a community deeply rooted in community service or education; one where few people spend any time online or everyone is verbose.

Does your profile accurately represent you?

Konstantin Guericke referred me to LinkedIn's marketing department to develop a slide deck to show my military peers the value of the platform. One set of peers were military officers, the other baby-boomers that grew up without technology in their hands. The most important concept to convey was that LinkedIn was not a fraud out to steal their identity. This was built post-bust of the dot-com boom. People were skeptical of web-based dot-com companies.

The real value proposition of LinkedIn is that it gives You the ability to convey the richness of your experiences with a story. ***The power to tell a story to win is important.*** *(See Tell to Win by Peter Guber.)*

With 5 or 35 years of experience, there is no place better to really convey the story of your professional life. It is an excellent place to showcase all your skills and abilities.

Even to this day, people ask me when they are "done" with LinkedIn. My response: anytime you can write 10 to 12 different, yet accurate and agreeing resumes in a strict copy-paste from a profile, you won't need LinkedIn anymore. And when you find a place to network with your peers and others in such a way that engenders trusted relationships. You won't need LinkedIn anymore. And when you find a place to share your thoughts on any variety of professional topics, to write and publish op-eds, and to engage in public dialog with others about the same, you won't need LinkedIn anymore.

"If it is not on your LinkedIn profile, you have never done it."
Joe Frankie

And if you can find a place to allow you to do all three, with over 600 million other professional people on the planet, you really won't need LinkedIn anymore. Because tomorrow, you will learn something new, you will have helped someone, you will have developed a new skill, and you will need to decide whether you want to capture that experience on your profile. People often think of their LinkedIn profile as a finite activity.

"Since the only constant is change, creating your LinkedIn profile is a journey rather than a destination."

Joe Frankie

Whether you are transitioning from the military into a civilian career or from a non-traditional job into a corporate role, you are likely progressing, or hoping to move into something better and more rewarding than you are doing now. So, now is the time to refine your story of the greatness you have to offer and to showcase your community and interests in the online space.

Even if you're a company executive and haven't written more than a website bio in the last fifteen years, you now must be found by more people than the retiring executive recruiter you've previously depended on. Business unit leaders know how to use LinkedIn.

Today's recruiters are not successful without being on it. Yes, networking still happens in the boardroom and beyond. But your networking is incomplete, less effective, and dwindling every year without the professional exposure and credibility you get from a polished LinkedIn profile, even less so without spending a few quality minutes each day on the platform.

The inevitable fact post-2015 is that you need to recognize your profile for what it is: the virtual reality of you, networking in the biggest networking event on the planet. It's been growing and going strong since its inception in 2003. Isn't it time you figured it out?

You can still find what you want without LinkedIn. But rather than your search taking about one month for every $10,000 of salary you seek, you can cut that time by half or more just by uber-scaling your networking using this important platform.

So how will you approach it? With the grace and measure of calculation required, or as a mere "I guess I should be there" blasé attitude? That will indicate to you whether you should proceed or not. I honestly hope that you do accept the power of this tool and that you will be open to some critique, advice and encouragement along the way.

If a retired military-trained, battlefield-hardened retired colonel can taste it, tweak it, take it for a test drive and make it work for myself and hundreds of executive clients, maybe you can, too.

Take 5!

This exercise will help you define your introduction in the next section.

What are some unique ways you have learned important life lessons?

What experiences have helped shape your critical decision-making skills that will help you to be even more successful in the future?

Your LinkedIn profile is *YOUR UNIQUE* story! Skills can be taught. What are the stories of your experiences and the problems you solved, the hurdles you overcame, the achievements your team reached together? How has that helped you learn how to focus your talents? How will that impact the potential for your success in the role you want to play in the future?

And that is how you change your perception. That is how you come to believe in yourself and your ability to network in five minutes or fifteen.

No matter who you are, what your experiences are, what your goals are… you absolutely MUST believe you are worthy and that you can achieve the recognition of your worthiness through this process. You must write truthfully about who you are. Be honest with yourself first. Recognize where you want to go next and what you bring to the table now. What problems have you solved?

"If you know where you are now and where you want to go— you can build a LinkedIn bridge to get there."

Joe Frankie

That's it.

If you do not believe yourself to be worthy, then put this book down. Visit www.loriruff.com to download a free copy of her 7th book "Keep It Real". That book will help you put your life into perspective, pare your perception to reality, and find some area of your life in which you indeed feel "worth it." Then come straight back here and let's get to work!

If you believe that you are worthy; if you believe we can help you discover, uncover, and portray your worthiness in these pages, then read on. Because you will succeed. So, let's get to work!

"Some might say it makes sense for you to base your brand on skills or experiences or important parts of your identity. You've worked hard to develop them through hard work or they're reflective of key values you hold. But what if your brand is shaped, in others' minds, by factors outside your control? What if, regardless of your preferences, others insist on noticing something extraneous? The only solution is to recognize what others are seeing and take control of your brand."

Dorie Clark
Keynote Speaker, Best Selling Author
Reinventing You (quoted), *Entrepreneurial You,* and *Stand Out*
Ivy-League Educator
Corporate Strategic Consultant

Introducing You

By now, we hope you're convinced to engage on LinkedIn. Now it's time for you to prepare!

There are indeed numerous books on LinkedIn, many which include sections dedicated to crafting a great profile. In fact, Mike O'Neil and Lori Ruff wrote the most comprehensive book which became the industry standard. Yet, she's going to say something outrageous to you. What will help you most is a simplified resource like the LinkedIn Profile Guidesheet® provided in the back of this book along with an honest friend or colleague who knows you well and one who knows the place you want to be. Or hire a seasoned consultant like Joe Frankie who is skilled at helping you craft stories that showcase your successes, qualify your skills and quantify your results.

If you are going to be here, you have two choices: do it yourself or ask for help to craft the best *you* possible on this important career-enhancing, credibility-improving, content-crafting platform. It's all about the metrics: what have you done; how have you done it; how successful were you; why was it important; and will anybody back you up. Lori Ruff, The LinkedIn Diva has always had help, even if asking trusted colleagues to review and critique. Shouldn't you consider it, too?

Craft and write your story!

Not comfortable talking about yourself in that way? Get over it. The work world is screaming for people who can solve problems. It is about metrics—qualitative and quantitative. What are you going to do when you finally get that all-important interview? Shouldn't you figure that out before you are in an impromptu interview? You should always sound confident and polished instead of searching for the right words on the spot. Nothing says, "He's unprepared" like sounding unprepared!

Take 5!

Have you ever considered yourself unique?
Who are you when you're at your best?
How can you apply those best attributes and find an audience?
How can you apply your best attributes in your work life?

— Here's a Tip! —

Instead of trying to decide how to talk about yourself, listen to how others talk about you. When your boss introduces you to someone via email, what does (s)he say about you? When a connection writes a recommendation for you, what is the story they tell and what success do they highlight? What are your most appreciated hero qualities?

You may ask, "Can you get me in front of someone? Can you get me an interview?" Rather than a two to three-hour interview with two to three people, now you must do a virtual interview via LinkedIn. Joe Frankie may know you and know you have the experience, but if it's not on LinkedIn, it didn't happen. If prospective employers can't see it, they won't consider you as a viable candidate.

Networking for Career Enhancement or Advancement

We can start here since it is the most popular reason on the planet to network, especially when you add the secondary reasons people network!

In his executive search business, Joe Frankie conducts the first two levels of the search now via LinkedIn. On the LinkedIn Recruiter® product, you can sort by number of connections or recommendations. Why should recruiters invest due diligence in you if you haven't invested in yourself to make it easy for them to find you?

Before LinkedIn, everyone in HR and recruiting had to sort and sift through information. Now a properly populated LinkedIn profile does the work of the personnel clerk and supervisor. Properly populating your LinkedIn profile allows the recruiter to hit the Easy Button® on the search. Handing hiring professionals their research on a silver platter sends you to the front of the hiring line. It's not personal; it's human nature and good business for people to do their work as efficiently as they can.

Networking for... Well, Everything Else

We have used LinkedIn to:

- Find Board members

- Fill skilled volunteer positions
- Seek radio guests and interviewees for blog posts and articles
- Search for musicians
- Connect nearly two dozen Marines in Charlotte, NC for a Veterans Day gathering in 2008 with only 24-hours' notice
- Find the top twenty women and top ten most-connected Latinos on LinkedIn
- Locate potential hosts and sponsors for local networking events for cities during a cross country speaking tour

Now people you network with and people who network with you can access accurate, peer-reviewed information about you, your abilities and accomplishments in a structured and systematic way. And when the search takes them to your profile, your investment in great storytelling allows them to meet the closest thing to the real you possible.

RockTheWorld™ with your Online Presence: Your Ticket to a Multi-Platinum LinkedIn Profile was the first book dedicated to the fine art of dressing your LinkedIn avatar to resemble the true nature of your complete persona. Not just the resume, but the whole person that someone would meet in person. It began as just a section of Mike O'Neil's first book on LinkedIn dedicated to sales professionals.

Once Lori Ruff joined his firm, Integrated Alliances, and used her experience and expertise to begin fleshing out that section of the book, they quickly realized that, for anyone from sales trainee to sales director to benefit, it needed its own cover. It launched as the training manual for other LinkedIn trainers, recruiting firms, sales organizations, even consultants.

As LinkedIn has become recognized for its value in the marketplace, Mike and Lori stopped updating the book because they designed a dynamic resource, the **LinkedIn Profile Guidesheet**® (added as a resource in the back of this book). As the world has changed, they try to recognize positive opportunities to change with it. Opportunities like gifting many of the LinkedIn trainers and others mentioned earlier with a creative commons copyright to use and adapt the Guidesheet to ensure it helps the most people possible.

That's an example of a great Project or Publication, which is how you'll find it on Lori Ruff's LinkedIn Profile. If your profile needs work, hop over to Page 72 and go over our Profile Cheat Sheet, then come back and pick up where you left off!

Joe Frankie notes that some of the best people he has found as a retained executive recruiter have not been the people that he was able to present to prospective employers. And here's what he says:

"When I am hired by a company to find a given person or position, I am expected to produce someone who is ready to take the field and get in the game. Many people I have talked to have not prepared themselves to be reviewed, evaluated or chosen by a new employer."

"Often, they believe that their experiences has been successfully communicated to the recruiter or headhunter. What they don't realize is companies are going to research them via their LinkedIn profile, which is their primary online footprint. If you have not listed and cataloged your projects, your successes and your experiences in the eyes of prospective employers, it didn't happen; you haven't done it."

Since early 2008, Lori Ruff has been a speaker, radio host, consultant and national non-profit executive. The numerous ways she's had to use LinkedIn to network for herself, for clients, for her employer and for her community causes are too many to name. If you can think of a reason to network and connect, she's likely "been there, done that" with LinkedIn, including being on the receiving end of being found!

Joe Frankie and Lori Ruff both prepare executives the same way across the board. They talk with them about how to present themselves and remind them how employers or others are going to research and look at them. If an executive cannot or will not get ready to present themselves on LinkedIn, they will be passed over by companies and people who are looking. It's that simple.

Do you want to be found? Do you want to advance your career? Be ready and get prepared so that companies can find you, evaluate you, easily understand how you will help them be successful, and quickly hire you. It happens every day. It might as well happen for you!

So. If we have sold you on the importance of your profile; get it done!

"It ain't bragging, if you can back it up."

Dizzy Dean

*"Life is a succession of lessons which must be
lived to be understood."*

Thomas Carlyle

Setting Up Your Success

Do you want to know if someone is trying to reach you, or would you rather not hear from anyone interested in hiring or doing business with you?

We all would want to know! That's why dressing up your profile for success is so critical.

If you haven't done this OR if you know someone who hasn't, pay attention for 5 Minutes! This Drill could make a difference for you or for someone you care about. *Otherwise, just skip ahead to the next section.*

When you look at your profile, you'll find a line with your LinkedIn profile URL and "Contact Information." Click each in turn.

- Click the pencil or gear button that is offered to allow you to edit your LinkedIn profile URL. Make it personal. Rather than your name and dashes and other odd characters, craft your LinkedIn profile URL to be something you can put on a business card, in an email address, or on a resume. LinkedIn.com/in/LoriRuff (caps not necessary) is much easier to convey than linkedin.com/in/sammy-e-haggar-jr-7b37138

- Next click "Contact Info" then the pencil you'll see near your email address. Be sure to indicate a primary email address that both well represents you and is one that you access frequently. Include every email address that you can confirm (up to ten are allowed). ***In this context, "confirmed" means addresses you have an active user ID and password. (keep a list of old information if you have to!).*** And if you leave a company do NOT delete the email! Think about how many business cards are floating on desks around the globe that have your old email on it. Would it be nice for people to be able to reach you via LinkedIn, even if they have an old address?

The Primary email address is important. Ensure it is one of your personal email accounts.

While you may want your company email to be your primary email address on LinkedIn, if you change it, you must manually change your email on all your groups. It's best to use a personal email for your LinkedIn profile unless you're in sales or business-development. Although not impossible, it is a time-consuming affair to re-affiliate everything to a new primary email address, re-populate contacts to a new service, and convert your life to a personally driven dashboard rather than using a corporate outlook account. Think seriously about what your primary email address should be for various needs.

"Yes, recruiters and HR professionals like to hit the Easy Button as often as possible."

Joe Frankie

Not convinced yet? Joe Frankie has a close friend who spent his career with a major oil company. Throughout his career, he had mixed his personal persona and business persona. He used his oil company email address for years as his primary email everywhere, including LinkedIn. Everyone he knew contacted him via his business email because he didn't maintain a personal account. He saw no need to have two.

As he approached retirement, he created a new personal account and Joe encouraged him to seek help from IT months before he retired. He needed a way to ensure he divorced his business from his personal contacts to make an easy transition on retirement. The time came but it was still a difficult affair since he had used his company email address for many online services, including LinkedIn.

Be authentic. Be real. Be human. Network, and build Communities because... a Network gives you Reach, but a Community gives you Power. #RonR... #NoLetUp!

Ted Rubin
Chief Marketing Officer, Photofy
Best Selling Author, Keynote Speaker
Return on Relationship, and *The Age of Influence: Selling to the Digitally Connected Customer*

Connecting You

Let's go further in preparing you to network super-efficiently. You want to spend more time in conversation that moves your needle than you do in research. While the research is essential, we like to minimize the time it takes to do it so you can focus on building relationships that lead to business.

You're not going to believe us right away but hear us out. You need to follow companies on LinkedIn. If you're interested in doing business with or working for some companies, and you follow them on LinkedIn, you'll not only be able to research their profile and organization, you'll receive regular updates in your home feed. That will give you mental nudges to stay aware of what's important to them.

If you engage with those updates—like or comment on them—more of their followers and, more importantly, more of their business leaders, will become aware of you. How? When a company posts anything on LinkedIn, if their social media team is a crack team (the number of those is increasing), they will send an email to all relevant executives and business leaders, alerting them to the post with a request to like, comment and share it to their networks and groups. You comment, they see your comment, they become aware of you too. Get the picture?

---

*"Don't just join the conversation as a listener; be actively engaged. Let people **see** you are there. **Say** something!"*

Lori Ruff

If you have not yet built a strong personal network, start first with following companies where you are interested in working or with whom you want to do business, so you get more of their updates in your home feed.

Take 5!

Who do you want to include in your "community"?

What are they interested in that you like to talk about?

What else are you interested in and what do you want to say about it?

But really, what do you really CARE about? And what do you have to say that will make a difference in people's lives?

Now... who ELSE is talking about those very things? Who ELSE can you publicly have a civil and intelligent conversation with, even if you don't agree, even if you agree to disagree but respect professional differences of opinion based on different audiences?

NOW you are tapping into the power source, not completely plugged in but closer than you have ever been.

This is where you have conversations that are overheard by your audience AND theirs and both can see how you conduct yourself in the public arena. Both have a chance to see how your peers see you, and both see you as peers with the person you are engaging with, even if you don't see it yet!

Upward Career Mobility

a) Follow the types of companies you are interested in working with, either by name, industry, location, etc.

b) When you find virtual mentors (those whose careers you want to follow) and people with whom you want to connect, follow their employer too.

c) Above all, be strategic about whom you follow so you can read and engage with the updates of those people and companies that are most relevant to you.

d) At the same time, don't neglect the power of a large network that crisscrosses the segment or the sector! The famous six-degrees of separation can be trimmed to three with aggressively strategic network building on LinkedIn like Joe Frankie has engaged in; i.e., leadership, management, military and energy as he focuses on helping military veterans transition to civilian careers. If he has time, he also enjoys following oil and gas, science and technology, bioscience and healthcare. While his primary interest might seem broad, the choices he makes are shaped by his secondary interests. Therefore, you can see the importance of truly being specific of what you like, then chiseling into more specific interests, and then chiseling again into the specific companies or countries or market segments. Each pass hones your search and effectuates results you can work with.

Personal Brand Building

a) A special note here: since this is **Personal** brand building, it is important to only follow companies that align with your brand. If they don't, even if any of the remaining criteria apply, do not follow them or people will be confused believing that you support their ideals, morals, beliefs, etc.

b) Follow the companies of the influencers with whom you connect.

c)   Follow the companies of people who share your vision.

d)   Follow the companies with whom your audience aligns.

e)   Follow the companies that employ people in your audience (for speakers, authors, writers, influencers, actors, performers).

f)   Follow the companies with whom your brand naturally aligns. For example:

- If you're a chemical engineer, you'd follow The Dow Chemical Company as well as others to keep your thumb on the pulse of the industry.

- If you're in supply chain, you want to follow other companies that are up and down the line, vendors and customers. You also want to follow similar companies to keep an eye on best practices and shifts in the market.

- Yes, follow competitors, too. The reasons are too numerous to list, but begin with shifts in the market, new trends, competitive intelligence…

g)   Be strategic about whom you follow so you can read and engage with the updates of those people and companies that are most relevant to building your brand.

h)   And, again, don't neglect the power of a large network that crisscrosses the segment within the country or across the globe! It works here, too. The famous six-degrees of separation can be trimmed to three with aggressively strategic network building on LinkedIn. Lori Ruff has engaged in that resulting in her becoming the third most connected woman on LinkedIn!

Preparing to Change Sectors

a)   Follow companies whose primary focus is the sector in which you are interested.

b) When you connect with people who are in your desired industry sector or vertical, follow their employer too.

And again! Be strategic about whom you follow so you can read and engage with the updates of those people and companies that are most relevant to you.

Learning New Glossaries

Following and daily checking in with these companies will give you a better grasp of the "glossary" in the new arena. Every industry has their own acronyms or phrases that are meaningful to them.

For example,

a) a joint in Texas is still the little hole-in-the-wall bar down the street, while in California or Colorado it might mean something completely different.

b) a Coke to someone in New York is a soft drink, while in Southern Louisiana, coke is a solid byproduct derived when refining crude oil.

c) a recruiter's book of business equates to a salesperson's lead sheet of current and potential customers.

When you know exactly what you want… You have the company and position pegged… You see the job and you know the players…

It is critical to follow the company page, any leaders in the company, and people who surround that position two levels up and two levels down.

Strategically, you need to get ahead of the opportunity. So, use LinkedIn to engage and connect with the hiring managers for that role. And do it before the position is open!

a) Connect with whomever you can. Start by engaging in the same groups and connect with the people who were "also viewed".

b) It's super important for you to follow the companies that your target company does business with as well as those that are in the same industry, their competitors, and their clients or customers. In this way, when your opportunity arrives you are prepared and ready to engage. You will be able to talk like you are already in the position.

c) This is where relationships matter most, because the majority of roles are filled because "someone knows someone." Be that someone.

"Networking via LinkedIn daily updates is an essential component of the Daily 5-Minute Drill.

"Remember: this does not work if you do not check in. Checking in daily by reading AND commenting on just a few updates helps you stay informed and stay in front of your selected audience... and, it only uses one or two minutes of your 5-Minute Drill!"

Lori Ruff

Adding a daily visit to the companies you care most about is essential. Since the feeds for companies and people have now been combined, it can be difficult to catch the posts of companies or people that don't post often mixed into the posts of those that do.

To make this efficient and quick and to keep your 5-Minute Drill to 5 minutes, follow these steps:

a) keep a digital list of the companies you care most about and why, perhaps even categorizing them.

b) Each week prioritize your list. If you have 3-5, checking in on each daily isn't a problem but if your list creeps to 10 or 15 or more, that starts to push your 5-Minute Drill into 15! So, split the list into 2 or 3 parts and check in on a few M-W-F and the others T-T-S. Or if you must, split it into three, then you would do 1/3 each on M-T-W then repeat. You get the idea. If you're in sales and your list gets longer, you are just going to have to settle in for a 15-Minute Drill rather than 5, perhaps twice a day. But don't worry, it'll be worth it!

c) For the companies you sincerely want to do business with or work at, it is worth the time to follow the senior executives of the company and the managers of the business unit that you are interested in engaging. Join mutually relevant groups they are in. And comment on a few of the posts they publish. But, do NOT go wild and ask to connect to everyone and comment on every post and join every group and essentially cyber stalk them! Do not join groups that you are not truly interested in or know nothing about the topic. That is disingenuous and you will likely be called on it before you can learn enough to fake it.

And, that is how you #KeepItReal

Take 5!

If you're serious about your career, throw in a bonus 5-Minute Drill every now and again. "Take 5" once a week to be strategic about networking and business development, maybe Saturday morning with coffee.

Do targeted searches on LinkedIn and find appropriate people. Scan their profiles and look for things you have in common.

Invite them to connect or send an Inmail saying you'd like to have a brief conversation to learn more about them and their business (not pitching or to talk about your products and services!)

Are you connected on LinkedIn?

- If so, send a quick message saying you're looking forward to the meeting or call.
- If not, invite them to connect, and tell them you're looking forward to meeting them.

Scan their profile to learn more about them. You may find things they want or need. If so and you can help, offer to connect with people in your network, or give them valuable information without obligation that will help them. You will build a network of people always willing to help you!

Jan Wallen, Lifestyle Design
Website: www.JanWallen.com
Twitter: @TheJanWallen
Facebook: www.facebook.com/thejanwallen

"Recognize your profile for what it is: the virtual reality of you. And LinkedIn is your meeting place for the biggest networking event on the planet!"

Joe Frankie

"Don't forget that there's a real person on the other side of your technology."

Lori Ruff

Promoting You

Networking online will never replace the warm handshake when you meet someone at a live networking event. However, LinkedIn can maximize the effectiveness of those interactions as well as to foster engagements you likely would not otherwise have.

In her book *Lori Ruff on Suite Branding*, Jorge Ortega, global communications and marketing executive shares, *"You are as good as your clients—your clients are as good as you are."* So, think about joining groups who are talking about the topics or industries you are truly interested in exploring. Topics that, as we discussed earlier, are authentic to what you truly care about that will connect you to the audience you truly want to connect with.

Whether that audience is a particular company, sector or country is of no consequence. The methodology and YOUR INTENT are the same. You speak, act, react, and behave as you would if that person and twenty others were standing in the room with you.

This step is no different from finding the right conversations at a networking event. In fact, it is no different than finding the right networking event to begin with! Yet this step—creating a quick 5-Minute Drill that lets you effectively maximize your networking on LinkedIn—is where people often falter.

If you join groups to join conversations and there are no conversations in a group that you join, it seems to defeat the purpose and wastes your time. The only reason to join groups where there is not a lot going on or nothing but "spammy" posts, is to be a step closer to the people in those groups through messaging and passive search. There are so many groups like that, how do you find the most valuable?

Let's start with our purpose here, which is to find the most valuable groups for **conversation**. Being found is important, yes but more so sparking conversation with the right people: those with whom you want to build your network of quality personal relationships as you work your own personal daily 5-Minute Drill.

Follow a few great groups to find the type of people you seek as well that offer genuine conversations such as you'd find at a professional event. The people who frequent these groups are there to network and grow just like you.

These are the Key Indicators for groups that will offer you a measure of value in addition to basic professional networking, or that will offer you stronger connections with whom to network.

1) The groups foster "broad discussions on trends, technology, regulations and innovation…"

2) The group is run by a group of people "incentivized" to make it work, i.e., in the case of FMIP, a company team who serves the industry with whom they foster relationships.

3) There are group rules everyone is encouraged to follow, that the group admins enforce.

4) Professionals that you respect are also in the group.

5) The best groups are typically larger, although smaller niche groups, hyper-focused on one aspect can also bring you a ton of value.

Here's an example: *Food Manufacturing Industry Professionals*

This group is designed to broadly discuss trends, technology, regulations, and innovations that are impacting the food production industry. Topics may include: R&D, food packaging & design, ingredients, processing & manufacturing, logistics, food service, retail management, consumer trends, and more.

Please read the group rules before posting.

This group is powered by the team at Food Dive.

— *Here's a Tip!* —————————————————————

Networking and promoting yourself and your ideas in groups is powerful because of the additional benefits of information gathering, watching trends as well as the market movers and shakers you can quickly find—especially in niche markets or global communities comprised of a tightly focused professional discipline.

Another benefit is that it offers a form to test conversational material before you try it in the real world. A LinkedIn Group is where you can develop relationships with peers like yourself and also with people much like your best customers. Here is your chance to ask them—through messaging—their thoughts about any idea, any concept you want to test. Discover important market information or offer the same to them and get a glimpse into the mind of your collective clients... What important information could you discover?

Recommended Groups

Groups for Executives
HBR

The Harvard Business Review is an outstanding group for those with a corporate executive mindset.

CFO

The CFO Network is the #1 group for CFOs and executive financial and accounting leaders. Connect with senior executives at Director, VP & CFO levels to network, discuss, or find accounting and CFO jobs.

CXO

Senior Executive Exchange. The Senior Executive Exchange is an international LinkedIn group for top leadership in organizations to share information and exchange ideas.

CDO

CDO Club for Chief Digital Officers and Chief Data Officers. A networking and support group for Chief Digital Officers and Chief Data Officers, and other digital leaders with similar roles and responsibilities. (Only a few hundred people in the group, but a powerful networking experience awaits!)

CIO

The CIO Forum is facilitated by CIO.com for members of the CIO community to connect and collaborate, and to move their business technology initiatives and careers forward.

CTO

Chief Technology Officer (CTO) Network. This is a group for CTOs and other executives to expand their network of people and ideas.

CMO

The *Marketing Executive Network* is a community for CMOs, brand managers, and digital marketers.

COO

The Executives Group is for Senior Executives: CEO, COO, CFO, CMO, CTO & All CXO's.

Groups by Sector/Vertical

Marketing

Media & Marketing Professionals Worldwide offers a big picture viewpoint from a worldwide community .

Energy

Linked:Energy. Those with Energy Industry Expertise will find this a heavily moderated haven.

Financial Industry Professionals focused on Technology

Financial Technology Group (FinTech) A group full of members in the Finance industry subsector of technology.

Not-for-Profit Sector

Young Nonprofit Professionals Network. A great group focused on building value for the non-profit professional.

Logistics/Supply Chain

The Logistics & Supply Chain Networking Group.

Food Manufacturing

Food Manufacturing Industry Professionals with more than 35,000 members is an industry behemoth.

Communications/PR

Public Relations and Communications Professionals. A group of Public Relations and Communications Professionals dedicated to increasing networking and business opportunities for its members. This group is (lightly) moderated.

Sales/Business Development

Sales and Business Development Professionals. This group is for experienced sales and business development professionals who understand next generation technology's impact on their profession and endeavor to continue learning and sharing.

Accounting

CPA & Business Professional Group officially sponsored by the American Institute of Certified Public Accountants (AICPA), connects CPAs, AICPA members and other affiliated professionals.

Engineering Groups

Representing hundreds of thousands, if not millions of professionals working in one of four major branches of engineering, each with their own subdisciplines, plus a broader interdisciplinary branch covering over 20 additional subject combinations, not all of which are a part of engineering in and of themselves!

As one would expect on LinkedIn, the variety of groups for each discipline, subdiscipline, and interdisciplinary branch as well as the profession collectively, result in nothing short of "numerous" ... already exceeding 20,000. A few token samples include:

- *Computer & Software Engineering Professionals* is for hardware and software engineering topics.(...for degreed professionals only)
- *Engineering Skills* (formerly Engineering Wall). Their dream is to deepen the skills of engineers and the engineering discipline and provide a free platform for young and experienced engineers alike to show their passion for the field.
- *CSCE The Canadian Society for Civil Engineering* ... look for groups administered by the associations, organizations, societies, and, in particular, licensing and/or credentialing organizations to which you belong.

Groups by Demographic

Veteran Groups

Like Engineering, there are many active and veteran military groups to choose from, likely reserve and guard as well. These are the largest (there are over 1,000) with many being specific to state or industry. Be selective, yes, but give any group you join a chance to produce results before you jump ship! Perhaps reach out to the group owner or manager(s) or ask some of the more active and engaged people to connect essentially as "virtual mentors."

- *US Military Veterans Network,* www.linkedin.com/groups/50953
- *US Veterans,* www.linkedin.com/groups/87020

- *Army Veterans*, www.linkedin.com/groups/47803
- *Veterans Hired*, www.linkedin.com/groups/3754418
- *We Hire Heroes—Veterans Employment and Business Group*, www.linkedin.com/groups/3754418

Professional Women

CitiConnect Professional Women's Group, a collaboration between Citi and LinkedIn to provide consistent value; it is heavily moderated.

Latino & Hispanic Professionals

ALPFA (Association of Latino Professionals For America). Through professional and student membership, ALPFA empowers and develops Latino men and women as leaders of character for the nation, in every sector of the global economy. They offer leadership development, networking, mentorship and community engagement.

Got that? Great!

"There can be no progress if people have no faith in tomorrow."

John Fitzgerald Kennedy

"When I let go of what I am, I become what I might be."

Lao Tzu

The Sword, the Saber, and the Scalpel

As you develop a routine around the template you have begun up to this point, Joe Frankie recommends you "use LinkedIn like a sword, a saber, and a scalpel." Here is what he means:

1) Like a Sword: Start with *RockTheWorld™ with LinkedIn v2.1*, this is the body of knowledge to take your sword and cut a broad swath...Who do I want to be on LinkedIn? How do I want to represent myself?

2) Like a Saber: Show up in the right places and engage the right people. Networking on your home page and in groups, even on company pages, is critical!

3) Like a Scalpel: Find the right people on LinkedIn to invite into to your world: "Who do I want to spend more time with?" Connect and engage them when they post or comment on someone else's post. Few people do; so, they will notice when you do!

Many executives and transitioning military seek help with LinkedIn. The challenge is quickly helping them understand the scope of what they are trying to achieve and the levels that they need to go through to achieve their desired results.

Using **RockTheWorld with LinkedIn v2.1** will assist them to learn basics (101) and progress through the intermediate level (201) and how to use this powerful tool to achieve their objectives, e.g.; transition from the military, transition between executive positions, transition between sectors, etc.

When you just start using LinkedIn it is like picking up and using a sword. It is a broad instrument and you control it with your arms and whole body. In the beginning with LinkedIn you need to learn the general rules and how it works. You begin to harness the power of LinkedIn as you build your network of friends, associates, and people who know you. You also learn that building good content is key to progressing. You are introducing yourself via a virtual conversation to other people.

Now that you have the basics you begin to interact on LinkedIn and you begin to harness the power of groups, receiving and giving endorsements and recommendations to those you know well. At this point you are progressing through LinkedIn 201 and you are using LinkedIn like a saber. You have a world-class headline, good content in your summary and experience sections, and you are continuing to build all facets of your profile. You are beginning to deftly thrust your profile (your LinkedIn persona) like a saber. You know what you need to do and where you are headed. You have learned the etiquette to move forward.

You have progressed through the body of knowledge on LinkedIn laid out in ***Rock The World with Linked v2.1***. You have been rewarded and learned who and how to connect with others you do not know directly. If you are a professional, you are using the first level of the Premium service to fully use the power of LinkedIn's reach and network in your world. You now have the power to cut through the network layers in the civilian world and start a conversation or introduce yourself to decision-makers you would not have access to normally—decision-makers, hiring authorities, and others. This is using LinkedIn like a scalpel. A very specific, targeted and precise way of doing so.

 Daily, check on 3-5 groups and do nothing more than liking AND <u>commenting</u> on a few discussions. It's not important that you post to be heard. Rather, that you comment to let others know that you heard them.

Try to join no more than 3-5 groups a week so you are not overwhelmed with checking in. Get used to the flow of each group, what you like about it, what kind of response or recognition you receive to help you select the next set of great groups to join.

Please note the process and description used to matriculate you from 101- the sword to 301-the scalpel. There are no shortcuts. No one will let you take sophomore English until you pass Freshman English. It is more of a journey than a destination and yes, LinkedIn is growing day by day; it is not static, either. We spend this time with you because you would not want a loved one having surgery where a doctor uses a sword for a surgical procedure. We do see people daily try to use LinkedIn as a sword wanting to have scalpel results. It does not bode well for their desired results.

Join groups!

a) When you join a group, your primary email is attached as the "notification email" for that group.

b) To change the email where you receive notifications, visit your group settings at the top right of each group. Look for a gear or a link indicating: "Your Settings"

c) When you connect with "virtual mentors", movers and shakers, look at the groups they are in and join those that are relevant for you and are also active. People hang out with people most like themselves.

"Thanks for connecting. As a quick intro, I own Crandall Stats and Sensors. We manufacture pneumatic HVAC sensors, controls, relays, and more. We sell direct and through distribution. Enough about me. Feel free to send me a short intro on what you do. Thanks!"

Mike Crandall
Entrepreneur and President
Crandall Stats and Sensors
www.crandallmfg.com

The "5-Minute Drill for Networking Success" Review

Does This Really Work? Let's Give it a Go! But first ask yourself, "**Do you respect your audience? Are you willing to spend personal time with them?**" Lori Ruff suggests that if your audience makes you frown when you wake up, it's time to start looking for renewed joy with a new audience or a fresh conversation that will spark your interest and electrify your wakeup call!

First prepare. Set a timer. For best results, use your mobile device's timer for your entire drill for each section. As you find your groove, use the stopwatch and hit Lap as you begin the next step and the next, so you know how much time you spend on each. Don't be afraid to modify the steps to suit you but hold off on that until you have completed at least ten days on the standard drill to give each step a fair shot

1) Open LinkedIn and scroll down your home page, full of updates and activity from personal connections and companies you follow. (**2 minutes**)
   a) Like and <u>Comment</u> on 5 - 20, depending on the size of your network and the length of your "Drill." Remember it is important to be seen as an intelligent human that cares about the people and the business. Don't leave throw-away comments, rather take a couple more seconds to invest in something a bit more intellectual and competent.

b) Be sure to take note of any immediately beneficial content or connections you come across. Write them down and bookmark the page.

c) But do NOT stop your drill! It is essential that you use your drill time on the drill—it's only Five Minutes! And you might miss an even bigger deal if you quit the race too early.

2) Visit 3-5 groups each day and find 3-5 active discussions you can <u>Intelligently</u> <u>Comment</u> on. People who posted the discussion will be seen but people who post comments to those discussions will be heard and make the original posters feel heard. Onlookers in the group will take notice of you as well, increasing your visibility from others "in the room" making you the topic of conversation. (**2 minutes**)

3) Look for and connect with at least two to five individuals every day. No executive must think long to come up with realistic options representative of at least two of the following categories. Be sure to send them a note if possible, either with the invite, via email, or even text. (**1 minute**)

a) Colleagues and peers.

b) Mentors and those whose work you admire.

c) Professionals you might meet at a conference and engage.

That's it. Notice how your network grows, your views increase, and, particularly as you refine the topics of your conversations, you become a recognized thought leader in your industry and for your discipline or area of expertise!

"Don't just tell us about what you're doing; tell us what you think about what you're doing.
It's one thing to share what you are doing on social media, but what most people are looking for is a human connection. It's not only appropriate to share your thoughts and feelings about what you are doing, it helps connect you with your followers and fans."

Joel Comm
NY Times Best Selling Author, Keynote Speaker
Twitter Power, Social POETRY, et al
Serial Entrepreneur, Brand Influencer
Gets to the Future First
Knows how to have fun!

Building and Nurturing Your Network: A Case Study

Listening to someone talking or reading about developing and nurturing your network is fine. But then you must sit down and do it and neither Lori Ruff nor Joe Frankie are there to look over your shoulder or answer questions.

So, let's walk through a practical case study together. We asked our friend and colleague, Bob Bowden, a typical seasoned professional by today's standards with experience in marketing and communications in multiple industries including financial services, banking, and consumer goods for a targeted research project and asked him to report what he learned.

*Note that, although all three believe strongly in the power of **Networking**, each have different needs and different ways to approach **Connecting**, i.e., accepting a LinkedIn invitation from people along the spectrum of who you know, how well, and in what context. We have found this to be driven in part by your need for a far-field reach and your tolerance for risk among other factors.*

Setting the Stage

LinkedIn is a powerful research tool that (surprise!) is a virtual networking environment. Imagine a portal that opens into a global space. It is, above all a place for connections. LinkedIn provides a range of ways to make those connections and to nurture the relationships you make there.

We have discussed all the ways that you can present yourself on the platform, individually, in industry or special interest groups and by sharing what you're thinking about in posts or comments. Please be reminded that the "gold" in LinkedIn is the relationship network that you grow and nurture. Your guiding principles for building your LinkedIn are yours and should align with your objectives.

If you are a recruiter, you will build a network of prospects, possible prospects and companies. You may or may not know all your connections. Indeed, you may have only had a quick message exchange with a given contact during the "connecting" introduction.

In sharp contrast, if you are focused on a local presence, your network may be limited to a more intimate group of contacts that you interact with frequently.

The point is that it doesn't matter where you fall on this spectrum and you can change your mind as your interests evolve. In the example of the local network, this may build in time to include out of state or out of country contacts who are considering the same kinds of issues who share their ideas with you in conversations via LinkedIn groups.

— **Here's a Tip!** —————————————————

Our advice is to be intentional about your network building and align it with your objectives. That is more important than building an enviable number of connections to brag about!

With your now clearly defined networking objective in mind, here is a sample career search case study to showcase the tools to help you grow and cultivate your LinkedIn network. The purpose of this case study is to identify and suggest some possible strategies for using the tools to organize and reach out to the greater LinkedIn universe. Use this as a starting point and a launch pad for your own thinking and experimentation!

As you review this case study, remember that it assumes that you have followed all our earlier advice and you have created some connections, identified and joined some groups and maybe even posted content a time or two. If you have only begun to get involved, consider these suggestions to supercharge your outreach.

Case Study Target

Identify an executive who left a large financial institution to start a new business on her own. Success is defined as someone who once had a large marketing department and who needs help building her new brand and awareness for her new products and mission.

Connections:

Reach out to current connections for names of possible opportunities. Focus on your connections in marketing, finance or small business owners. This section could include individuals, groups, companies or even hashtag interests. We will start with your current contacts and make comments about how to add/ enhance new contacts.

- Before you contact anyone, determine in measurable detail what you are looking for. Think about what a successful contact would be. Are you looking for a contact who owns their business? One who works in a given industry? Or are you flexible? Would you rather work with a younger or older workforce? The better you describe what success looks like for you, the better—and more likely—people are to help you.

- Use measurable detail—not just financial businesspeople but family office or insurance solutions officers working with clients in the Southeast. How detailed you get is determined by how you define your success, so give it some thought. A suggested start might be a family office in Virginia or North Carolina who work with established families to define and execute their income, charitable and estate strategies. The ideal candidate would want to develop a plan to identify potential clients, resources in related fields, and create awareness and interest in working with the family office professionals. Going forward, potential connections might include estate and tax attorneys, real estate professionals, banking and or health care contacts as well as potential family clients.

- Under the My Network tab (look at the menu ribbon at the top of your LinkedIn page), you will find all your connections. When you have defined what your ideal contact opportunity is, review the list for possible resources to reach out to and to ask for references or referrals.

- Use the filter function at the top of the first page of connections. You can filter by location, job, school, industry company and even content (date of post, job title or even by <u>what is being said about you by connections</u>). Filters can help focus your search. You might make your first cut include all connections within Virginia and North Carolina. You could then look at your connections in the related job categories.

- In addition to your current connections, you can also look for new contacts. In the left banner on your Home page, there are two or three clickable headings. Everyone has Who's Viewed Your Profile. You might see

Grow Your Network. These links suggest possible new connections for you that a) help build your network and b) create new opportunities. Click and review that link periodically, perhaps once or twice a week!

— **Here's a Tip!** ——————————————————

If someone helps you write any part of the narrative of your profile, be sure YOU edit and polish the final version that gets posted onto LinkedIn. It is your voice that should be heard online, over the phone, and in person. If the cadence, the phrasing, or the tone does not match, people may not trust you and they won't know why.

You've had that uneasy feeling before. Something felt off but you couldn't put your finger on it. Don't let that happen to you. Take the time to be sure your voice print is what the reader hears everywhere.

———————————————————————

- The Who Reviewed Your Profile link might show an opportunity that you would like to follow up. Click on the ones who interest you. You might connect or send a note asking for more information about what they are looking for depending on your level of interest and whether they fit into your network objective and align with your brand.

- Grow Your Network (*also can be reached from My Network on the Menu Ribbon across the top of your screen*) suggests similar links to your current connections. You may see invitations in the top row followed by people you've worked with, shared a school, business experience or any mutual connections. Again, you can research these suggestions by clicking to see their work experience and what they may have posted to see how they might improve your network.

- Your Network Growth page also has sections to suggest links to companies and hashtags. At the very bottom of the page, there are More Connection suggestions. These suggestions include people, groups, companies and hashtags. Following any of these items adds more information for LinkedIn to make better recommendations for you and it adds additional search information detail.

- Like any other contact, you should click on these suggestions and review what the page is all about. What do they discuss? What content is considered or shared and who visits. You can even see how many of your current connections follow the same pages. The company pages generally include a link to the company website to further help your research.

- Don't be afraid to reach out to any contacts you discover in this process. Much like meeting someone at an onsite networking event, you never know what you may find if you stay open. We suggest that you be alert to how the new contacts might help other members in your network or how you might make an introduction that offers value to this new connection.

- When you do reach out, think about your audience. Assuming your connections are friends or work colleagues you know well, you can outline your description of what you are looking for and ask if they know anyone or anyone else you should meet. You can offer a chance to discuss this over coffee or lunch if that is more comfortable. If the connection is someone you have not met or reached out to before, suggest a quick phone call or ask for a convenient time to call. If they offer a time, call and remember to be respectful of their time! If it goes well, you can schedule a second, more in-depth conversation. Think about your audience and be respectful!

- Follow up on any ideas and, if people have made a referral for you, it's always a good idea to get back to the them and thank them whether you hit pay dirt or not. A quick message on LinkedIn or text (if appropriate) shows your appreciation and respect. A written note is the gold standard.

Be selective with the groups, companies, and connections on your target list. It's better to have a few you check regularly–no less than once each week for your active list and have lists that you touch once a quarter and at the least twice a year

Leave groups and unfollow companies or unfollow (perhaps even disconnect from) connections that are not aligned with your purpose unless you want a soft affiliation to other connections through that group, company or connection.

Then there are those connections that I, Lori, have not talked to in several years, but we circle back around to bring value back into each other's lives... some even eight years later! Until I have a reason to say, "Goodbye" I tend to give people the benefit of the doubt. That policy has served me well. Perhaps it will you, too.

Groups:

Have you found/joined any Groups? Are there any possible opportunities in any Groups you belong to? You might ask a direct question of the group or follow up with any names/comments posted who seem to be looking for the expertise you offer.

- Your Groups are shown in the left column of your page. In addition, there are recent and popular hashtags that you are following. Use the hashtags to both guide your search and to identify new groups who are interested in what you are interested in and who are discussing ideas that you admire.

- Check in with your groups regularly. Listen to the conversation and discussion and comment as appropriate. By being involved and more importantly, engaged, you become known and you build your online reputation. If someone makes a comment that inspires you or makes you think, respond! More than that, the group is a great forum to ask for help in finding opportunities.

- Compared to an individual connection, a Group is less formal and a better environment to ask for help. The trick is to be strategic. If the group becomes a job posting board or if people just ask for leads and don't share meaningful ideas, the whole group collapses as members leave and avoid the site. If you have been contributing and adding value, it is appropriate to ask for help as you would ask at networking event.

- Here the message might be to ask open ended questions what do you think about (this area I am interested in pursuing)? Do you have any experience with (the area or people practicing in the area)? Use these questions to help guide and direct your search. You can research and even reach out to any names you get.

- Again, be strategic. Do you have anything in common with the group member or the potential opportunity that she identified? Talk about the common area and get to know the person before you shake them down for information! Treat your communication like you would if you met someone waiting in line for coffee or at a Little League game.

— **Here's a Tip!** —————————————————————

Be friendly! Joking aside, some people are just not friendly to people they do not know. If that's you, take a good look in the mirror and learn how to smile. That one skill will double your income twice as quickly as a scowl! (Look at Richard Branson. He is never NOT Smiling!)

- If you have started a conversation and established a relationship, it is far easier to talk about referrals or opportunities. And it is easier to find points of mutual benefit and find ways to help each other. Remember the main idea of a group is to bring like-minded people together so that all can benefit from shared ideas, resources and experience. Honor that obligation!

Job Post Tab:

LinkedIn provides a job bulletin board option in the blue banner at the top of the page. You can search by location or job title. This section can help you make sure you don't miss any opportunities where a potential employer might be searching for you!

- Type a job title or area in the Job box and choose a location. Job postings appear that you can save or set an alert for. (by clicking the Alert button at the top of the page)
- Characteristics in the Job box can be general (Marketing) or more specific. (Marketing Analyst or Marketing Assistant-Part Time)
- You can filter postings by location, mile radius from you, date posted, company or experience level required.
- Once you find an opportunity that interests you, you can save or apply by clicking the appropriate button under the posting.
- And remember this is LinkedIn! You can click on the company or person offering the position and start your research. Learn about the company, its products, their competition and your position and its contribution to the whole! Be prepared to ask and answer challenging questions!

LinkedIn Premium Upgrade:

Use LinkedIn Premium to identify potential owners in target industries. (e.g. marketing, finance, banking, insurance, investments or small businesses with a finance/marketing focus)

- By upgrading to Premium, you can search beyond your connections to find potential contacts.
- Premium allows you to search by industry, category, title, company and location.
- After you find a potential contact, review their profile for experience, capabilities and any points of common interest. These touchpoints are helpful as you look for points of contact.

- By using the People tab and the filters, you can explore for possible connections within your network so that you can ask for a referral or warm introduction.

LinkedIn® Profile *Cheat* Sheet

This (adapted) **LinkedIn Profile Guidesheet®** arms you with essentials for creating or improving your LinkedIn Profile with rapid results. It's adapted from the 188-page LinkedIn profile SEO book, ***Rock The World™ with Your Online Presence 2.1*** by Mike O'Neil & Lori Ruff, The LinkedIn Rockstars™.

So, let's get to work!

Fire up a word processor on your tablet or laptop. You will use it to craft your LinkedIn profile text to copy/paste. LinkedIn has no spell check capability and scrolling windows make data entry difficult.

While you are at it, Fire up LinkedIn as well. First, open your settings and set **Turn on/off your activity broadcasts** to OFF.

Next, open two tabs or windows, one in **Edit Profile** mode and one **View Profile** so you can switch between them, refresh or reload your page and instantly see how your text looks on the screen.

But don't stop there! Test it on your phone, too, and if you have an iPhone or Samsung, an LG, Motorola, or Huawei, be sure you ask a couple of friends or colleagues with other models to send you a screen shot or hand over their device for 15 minutes!

From the beginning of our careers, we have been taught and believed in the **FIT IN but *STAND OUT* principle.**

1) ***Fit In*** to get FOUND—SHOW UP in search results, more importantly, when you are found, you want to look like someone who will *Fit the Bill* they are trying to fill, *Fit In* to the corporate culture they want you to navigate. You get the picture. *Show up and be a shoo in!*

2) **Stand Out** to be the logical choice, the best choice, the defensible choice, the *gotta have* it choice selected from the lists, the choice to get the call, to one to make the deal!

   a) Not convinced? Why do schools have class standings, valedictorians, honors classes, programs, and distinctions such as summa cum laude, bachelor's degree with honours, and university medals?

   b) Still not convinced? The US military prides itself on breaking down individualism—to work as one team, one unit, one command—yet offers especially rigorous training for the chance to become yet again a part of the elite teams: the green berets, commandos, special forces, or Navy Seals. And individuals are awarded medals like the Purple Heart and the Distinguished Service Cross.

--- **Here's a Tip!** ---

Type your draft in a Word Processor and save your work! Then copy/paste to LinkedIn. Keying directly into the browser is problematic—you can't save progress as you type, character limitations, etc.

Remember: once you paste and save, view the result

Use special characters like these or copy them from other profiles to draw attention (just don't overdo it):

| ▌ ◊ ▶ ◀ ↔ ◆ • ★ ☆

Be sure to *view your profile* and test it after each change!

Name

Seems simple but this is a place to *Fit In*. Do not include anything but your **natural name and lettered credentials**. LinkedIn DOES lock your account when they find violations *[see User Agreement 8.1.c. You will "Use your real name on your profile." and 8.2.a. You will not "Create a false identity on LinkedIn, misrepresent your identity, create a Member profile for anyone other than yourself (a real person)].* They do not want the platform to look like a used car sales lot.

Don't be that person

Picture

Use what works best for Professional YOU. Just make it recognizable and interesting—and SMILE!

— A few examples

www.linkedin.com/in/mikeoneil
www.linkedin.com/in/ileanamusa3
www.linkedin.com/in/aquatialowens
www.linkedin.com/in/marketingprstrategist
www.linkedin.com/in/natalieboden

A simple, crisp headshot from your phone is great. Be sure you have good lighting and your face is in focus. A professional photo is great, too. A clean, white background is best, but many look amazing that don't follow the rules.

No Exceptions: no group photos, logos or replacing your image with pictures of your kids or pets… *This is NOT Facebook!*

Uploading and cropping are easy. The final image size is 400 x 400 pixels. (enlarged if someone clicks on your image to zoom in)

Headline (120 char.)

Your Headline is the 2nd most important field of your profile after your Name, which should ONLY include your name. Do not accept the default "Title at Company". Instead, use compelling, colorful words and formatting (**Career Definition Keywords | Keyword Rich Why Statement**).

This is your "Why" people choose to learn more about you.

About, formerly Summary (2,000 char.)

This is a conversation between you and your reader— although it is ABOUT you, this is your avatar! This should not be 3rd person. Who are you? How do you help others? How can they help you? Include a high-level overview of current, relevant information. Be interesting, a little personal with limited historical info.

End with a call to action. Now that you've been introduced, what should they do next?

Experience (100 Title/100 Co./2,000 Desc.)

Include all relevant intern, resident, fellowship, and paid positions to create connection and conversation opportunities. If the company has a LinkedIn company page, be sure you connect to that page. Properly done, the company logo from their page will appear next to their name on your profile.

Have you had multiple positions at one company? LinkedIn now connects those positions to show lateral and upward mobility.

Do NOT upload resume data.

List years only and note by default they will be listed chronologically by start date.

For each position, answer the following:

1) What does the company do?
2) Who do they do it for (customers)?
3) Where do they operate (territory)?
4) What was your role there?
5) What made you special, what did you do and learn then that will serve your clients better now? What did you accomplish that made you stand out, proving you could likely do it again?

Now, think about your actual and functional title. You have 100, keyword rich character spaces to work with. What do you think people will use to search for someone like you—no, not your glossary—what words will THEY use before they know you well, before they know what is brilliant about you?

Education (2,000 char.)

Not just for college: include college classes, business training (i.e., management), technical training (i.e., Cisco), and professional training (i.e., Dale Carnegie).

If you're young—or if you like the conversation starters—it's OK to list high school, if desired. Years only. Include special projects and educational and vocational activities.

Just like Company pages, be sure to connect to the school or company pages here as well. It will connect you to alumni.

Skills & Endorsements

Think about your Industry Knowledge, Tools & Technologies you use, and Interpersonal Skills. What other career specializations apply to you?

Interests

As you select people and companies to follow and groups to join, this is where all whom with you "affiliate" show up. *Protect your reputation; you never get it back!*

Again: Be Careful. If you want to "follow" someone that does not align with your brand, keep a list off LinkedIn of their name, URL, and why you're following them. Create categories, too. This will be a critical time saver during the daily "only" 5-Minute Drill!

Recommendations

If you want 5-15 recommendations. You might ask for 25-30. Kudos from customers and supervisors are best. Ask them to describe specifics of a project and your contribution to its success in just 3-4 sentences.

— *Here's a tip!* —————————————————

Get a Recommendation by GIVING a Recommendation!

Showcase Services

Not for everyone, but don't dismiss this if you don't run a business or you're not in sales! Look at how everything on LinkedIn can help you *Fit In and Stand Out!*

Choose one business focus and select the services that you offer.

Contact Settings

Include only what you monitor. People must be logged into LinkedIn to see this information.

Web Sites (Part of Contact Settings)

This feature isn't just for people who have something to sell or show off! Use all three available site listings—even subpages of the same site. Corporate? Link to your profit center, an info page about a major initiative, a collaborative effort with an industry partner, or a major NGO activity.

Do you support individually a non-profit such as Humane Society or ASPCA? Share the love. Are you an adjunct professor? Are your kids in a competitive sports league, marching band, or scouts? What areas of your life would you invite someone to learn more if it applied to them?

— *Here's a Tip!* —————————————————————

You get the idea. Look at how these "common place" tools might help you Stand Out a little further than the rest. Think of this as the equivalent of:

a) your site is furthering your business interests, or/and

b) your site is helping people get to know a little more about who you are, what you do after work—this is the "water cooler conversation" and best .

c) YOU are providing people who visit your profile a value-add by directing them to unexpected ***yellow-brick-road.***

If you list a non-traditional site use the label option "OTHER" and **write a custom label**. Instead of **Company** choose **Other** and type: "Dow Chemical is Hiring" or "SEI Home Page" or "PSI's Impact Blog" or "Girl Scouts of VA Skyline Council".

Adding New Sections

LinkedIn makes new types of information optional so explore the "Add profile section" link in your header or, as you scroll down your profile, it should pop up under the menu bar.

Skills, Certifications & Publications are popular but explore the space! This is a place for Professional Networking.

Rather than get more disconnected from real people as we get more connected to our technology, everything that LinkedIn—everything Lori Ruff and Joe Frankie espouse is designed to help you showcase your profile and help you network to enable richer connections with real people in the real world.

— *Don't Forget!* —

Complete LinkedIn 101 with Rock the World™ with LinkedIn: v2.1, by Mike O'Neil & Lori Ruff available on Amazon.

About the Authors

Lori Ruff is internationally celebrated as "The LinkedIn Diva," beginning with the iconic release of *RockTheWorld™ with Your Online Presence: Your Ticket to a Multiplatinum LinkedIn Profile* in 2009. She co-hosted *RockTheWorld™ with LinkedIn* radio with Mike O'Neil, The LinkedIn Rockstar 2010-2014.

She is a world-class Brand Influencer, Social Engagement Strategic Advisor, engaging speaker and intriguing analyst. She has worked with corporate and government brands and executive top performer programs. Lori's expertise helps you foster positive online relationships and increases your bottom line for less.

You know Emotional Intelligence is supposed to work but does anybody really use that stuff? She feels... she loves... she laughs... she shares... she helps... she finds joy... She is driven and seeks to be fulfilled by helping to fulfill others. She is certainly an out of the...wait, there are boxes?!

She has been dubbed "The Heart of Social Media" who attracts those tired of hearing the same old data and the same old solutions to the same old problems. Lori's recommendations are very different but somehow make perfect sense. Why haven't you tried that before? "Because," LinkedIn asserts "there is never an advantage to following the crowd—especially in marketing when the crowd is usually wrong." LinkedIn's Global Leads of Market Development espouse contrarian ideas in B2B marketing—little-known best practices that offer a significant edge over your competition.

- They assert that more data often leads to worse outcomes. Lori practices following her educated instincts because she takes the pulse of the dynamic if vulnerable authenticity vein of the online vs real life community connection.
- They assert—and she practices—targeting non-buyers of your products and she helps you design an effective outreach program.
- They assert—and she practices—how to choose "impersonalized" but authentic creative over "personalized" yet unimaginative creative to capture and engage your audience on time.

Want help?
LinkedIn.com/in/loriruff

Just have a couple of questions?
Clarity.fm/loriruff

Joe Frankie is a West Point graduate who had a full career in the U.S. Army as a warfighter and logistician for 30+ years. He commanded at all levels from platoon thru installation. Post military, he used his logistics skills to work on infrastructure projects in the US and internationally.

Currently, as an author, coach, and search consultant he advises military veterans and executives. He claims over 40 years of leading multifunctional teams worldwide in engineering, logistics, life sciences, technology, aviation and environmental services from startups to Fortune 500 companies in both private and public sectors.

Joe lives near Houston, Texas with his wife, Karen and their Miniature Schnauzer, Ollie. Lori lives in Central Virginia nestled near the Blue Ridge Mountains but can often be found on a train traveling through Washington, DC or into New York.

Need Joe now?

LinkedIn.com/in/joefrankieiii

Press In

Look us up
www.5-minutedrill.com

Follow Joe on
LinkedIn: linkedin.com/in/joefrankieiii
Twitter: twitter.com/joefrankieiii

Follow Lori on
LinkedIn: linkedin.com/in/loriruff
Twitter: twitter.com/loriruff
Facebook: facebook.com/linkedindiva
Instagram: instagram.com/loriruff

And look for more books by 5-Minute Drill Press … *because your time has <u>meaning</u>!*

Titles Worth Your Time

The Age of Influence: Selling to the Digitally Connected Customer
By **Ted Rubin** (The Rubin Organization)

Bury My Heart at Conference Room B: The Unbeatable Impact of Truly Committed Managers
By **Stan Slap** (Penguin (USA) LLC)

Impact: How to Get Noticed, Motivate Millions, and Make a Difference in a Noisy World
By **Ken McArthur** (Career Press)

Leadership Lessons of the White House Fellows: Learn How To Inspire Others, Achieve Greatness and Find Success in Any Organization
By **Charles P. Garcia** (McGraw-Hill Education)

Mustang The Story: From Zero to $1 Billion
By **Bill Higgs** (MustangTheStory.com)

Mutuality Matters: How You Can Create More Opportunity Adventure & Friendship With Others
By **Karé Anderson** (sayitbetter.com/book)

Rites of Passage at $100,000 to $1 Million+: Your Insider's Lifetime Guide to Executive Job-changing and Faster Career Progress in the 21st Century
By **John Lucht** (Viceroy Press)

Tell to Win: Connect, Persuade, and Triumph with the Hidden Power of Story
By **Peter Gruber** (Crown Business)

Time to Think: Listening to Ignite the Human Mind
By **Nancy Kline** (Cassell)

The Virtual Handshake: Opening Doors and Closing Deals Online
By **David Teten** and **Scott Allen** (AMACOM)

Words that Sell: More than 6000 Entries to Help You Promote Your Products, Services, and Ideas
By **Richard Bayan** (McGraw-Hill Education)

More Titles by/with Lori Ruff

#ENTRYLEVEL TWEET Book02: Relevant Advice for Students and New Graduates in the Day of Social Media
By **Christine M. Ruff** and **Lori Ruff** (THINKaha)
Lori Ruff on Suite Branding

#PRIVACY TWEET Book01: Addressing Privacy Concerns in the Day of Social Media
By **Lori Ruff**, Edited by **Rajesh Setty** (THINKaha at privacytweet.com)

RockTheWorld™ with LinkedIn v2.1: A Multi-Platinum Profile PLUS a Classic Rock Soundtrack
By **Mike O'Neil** and **Lori Ruff** (RockTheWorld Media Group)

RockTheWorld™ with your Online Presence: Your Ticket to a Multi-Platinum LinkedIn Profile 2nd Edition
By **Mike O'Neil** and **Lori Ruff** (Networlding)

Breaking Free: Overcoming Self Sabotage.
Edited by **Linda Ellis Eastman** (Professional Woman Publishing)

50 Seeds of Greatness.
By **Germaine Moody** et al (Become Endless Publishing)

Social BOOM!: How to Master Business Social Media to Brand Yourself, Sell Yourself, Sell Your Product, Dominate Your Industry Market, Save Your Butt, … and Grind Your Competition into the Dirt
By **Jeffrey Gitomer**, et al (FT Press)

Social Poetry: Boosting Engagement and Encouraging Conversation by Using Inspirational, Educational and Entertaining Photoquotes
By **Joel Comm**, et al (Joel Comm, Inc.)

The Young Professional Woman: Breaking Into the Business World & Succeeding.
Edited by **Linda Ellis Eastman** (Professional Woman Publishing)